This Bucket List Journal Belongs To:

_____

My Bucket List

Bucket List

What

Why

How

Completed

Date

Where

With

Notes/Thoughts/Memories

Would I Do It Again?

yes ☐   no ☐

Memories In Pictures

Souvenirs

Bucket List

What

Why

How

Completed

Date

Where

With

Notes/Thoughts/Memories

Would I Do It Again?

yes

no

Memories In Pictures

Souvenirs

Bucket List

What

Why

How

Completed

Date

Where

With

Notes/Thoughts/Memories

Would I Do It Again?

yes ☐   no ☐

Memories In Pictures

Souvenirs

Bucket List

What

Why

How

Completed

Date

Where

With

Notes/Thoughts/Memories

yes

no

Would I Do It Again?

Memories In Pictures

Souvenirs

Bucket List

What

Why

How

Completed

Date

Where

With

Notes/Thoughts/Memories

Would I Do It Again?

yes

no

Memories In Pictures

Souvenirs

Bucket List

What

Why _____ How _____

_____

_____

Completed

Date _____ Where _____

With _____

Notes/Thoughts/Memories

_____

_____

_____

_____

Would I Do It Again?

Memories In Pictures

Souvenirs

Bucket List

What

Why   How

Completed

Date   Where

With

Notes/Thoughts/Memories

Would I Do It Again?   yes   no

Memories In Pictures

Souvenirs

Bucket List

What

Why

How

Completed

Date

Where

With

Notes/Thoughts/Memories

Would I Do It Again?   yes ☐   no ☐

Memories In Pictures

Souvenirs

Bucket List

What

Why

How

Completed

Date

Where

With

Notes/Thoughts/Memories

Would I Do It Again? yes ☐ no ☐

Memories In Pictures

Souvenirs

Bucket List

What

Why

How

Completed

Date

Where

With

Notes/Thoughts/Memories

yes

no

Would I Do It Again?

Memories In Pictures

Souvenirs

Bucket List

What

Why

How

Completed

Date

Where

With

Notes/Thoughts/Memories

Would I Do It Again? yes ☐ no ☐

Memories In Pictures

Souvenirs

Bucket List

What

Why

How

Completed

Date

Where

With

Notes/Thoughts/Memories

Would I Do It Again?

yes

no

Memories In Pictures

Souvenirs

Bucket List

What

Why

How

Completed

Date

Where

With

Notes/Thoughts/Memories

Would I Do It Again?   yes ☐   no ☐

Memories In Pictures

Souvenirs

Bucket List

What

Why _____   How _____

_____   _____

_____   _____

Completed

Date _____   Where _____

With _____

Notes/Thoughts/Memories

_____

_____

_____

_____

_____

Would I Do It Again?   yes ☐   no ☐

Memories In Pictures

Souvenirs

Bucket List

What

Why   How

Completed

Date   Where

With

Notes/Thoughts/Memories

yes   no

Would I Do It Again?   □   □

Memories In Pictures

Souvenirs

Bucket List

What

Why _____   How _____

_____

_____

Completed

Date _____   Where _____

With _____

Notes/Thoughts/Memories

_____

_____

_____

_____

_____

Would I Do It Again?   yes ☐   no ☐

Memories In Pictures

Souvenirs

Bucket List

What

Why

How

Completed

Date

Where

With

Notes/Thoughts/Memories

Would I Do It Again?   yes ☐   no ☐

Memories In Pictures

Souvenirs

Bucket List

What

Why _____ How _____

_____

_____

Completed

Date _____ Where _____

With _____

Notes/Thoughts/Memories

_____

_____

_____

_____

_____

Would I Do It Again?   yes ☐   no ☐

Memories In Pictures

Souvenirs

Bucket List

What

Why _____   How _____

_____

_____

Completed

Date _____   Where _____

With _____

Notes/Thoughts/Memories

_____

_____

_____

_____

yes   no

Would I Do It Again? □   □

Memories In Pictures

Souvenirs

Bucket List

What

Why .... How ....

....

....

Completed

Date .... Where ....

With ....

Notes/Thoughts/Memories

....

....

....

....

....

Would I Do It Again? yes ☐ no ☐

Memories In Pictures

Souvenirs

Bucket List

What

Why _____ How _____

_____

_____

Completed

Date _____ Where _____

With _____

Notes/Thoughts/Memories

_____

_____

_____

_____

_____

yes no

Would I Do It Again? ☐ ☐

Memories In Pictures

Souvenirs

Bucket List

What

Why _____ How _____

_____

_____

Completed

Date _____ Where _____

With _____

Notes/Thoughts/Memories

_____

_____

_____

_____

_____

_____

yes

no

Would I Do It Again? ☐   ☐

Memories In Pictures

Souvenirs

Bucket List

What

Why   How

Completed

Date   Where

With

Notes/Thoughts/Memories

Would I Do It Again?   yes   no

Memories In Pictures

Souvenirs

Journal

Journal

Journal

Journal

Journal

Journal

Journal

Journal

Journal

Journal

Journal

Journal

Journal

Journal

Journal

Journal

Journal

Journal

Journal

Journal

Journal

Journal

Journal

Journal

Journal

Journal

Journal

Journal

Journal

Journal

Journal

Journal

Journal

Journal

Journal